IS THIS NEW HOLINESS SCRIPTURAL ?

REMARKS

SUGGESTED BY THE

CONFERENCE AT RED HILL,

JULY, 1875.

- —

LONDON:

W. MACINTOSH, 24, PATERNOSTER ROW.

PRICE ONE PENNY.

Preface.

THE object of this treatise is to give a brief account of that movement known as "SCRIPTURAL HOLINESS," and, while allowing that it embraces some truths dear to all evangelical Christians, to point out the errors and unscripturalness of its distinctive and special teaching.

From the addresses and writings of Messrs. R. Pearsall Smith, Boardman and others, I obtained some knowledge of their doctrines; but the subject came more under my notice at a three days "CONFERENCE," of which Admiral Fishbourne was Convener and Chairman, and where Dr. Asa Mahan and other recognised leaders, propounded and illustrated it.

Conscious of the liability of those who profess Christianity to overlook the practical bearing of its precepts, and their proneness to settle in the ruts of worldly conformity,—I would especially guard against any expressions that might seem to apologize for that carnality which is the bane of the Church. Surely the grace of God should influence all the life and walk of every Christian, so that each one can say " I will walk at liberty, for I seek thy precepts; " a liberty very distinct from the license of corruption, (ii. Peter ii. 19) or the looseness of an irresponsible Antinomianism.

The limits and design of this tract preclude any lengthy extracts or detailed criticisms. In a collection of Letters recently issued under the title of " The Brighton Convention and its doctrinal teaching * " [Nisbet: Macintosh—2d.] there is a list of publications in which the whole system is more fully reviewed.

T. ROWLAND HOOPER.

RED HILL,
    SURREY,
        August 24th, 1875.

THE (SO CALLED)

"Scriptural Holiness" Movement.

---◆---

MORE GRACE! INCREASED FAITH! GREATER LOVE! These have been the desires of saints down the long ages, and such prayers are never more timely than when the tide of open opposition to truth runs low, and silver slippers have become more fashionable than the pilgrim's "shoes of iron and brass."

Times of refreshing, revival, and reformation, have come from the presence of the Lord; and the church—the living family of God—has again and again "in the midst of the years,"— in the darkness of persecution and apostacy,—or in the sunshine of worldly favor,—found answers to her cry: "O Lord! revive thy work." But these good seasons have been interspersed with, and imitated by various movements, that apparent need, peculiar circumstances, or the ingenuity of their promoters, have called into existence; which appear in themselves so plausible, or conjoined with divine truths, become so deceptive, that Christians have been diverted, hindered, and perplexed even when not led into the intricate mazes of error.

Of this class is the present movement called by its promoters, "The Higher Christian Life;" "Scriptural Holiness;" "Full Consecration;"—and, by its opponents, "Perfectionism;" which (so amiable in its appearance and so unobjectionable in its early utterances) has proved to be a new or revised religious theory, having its systematic modes of teaching and principles of interpretation; and though at present very general and unattached, it appears likely to become at least a distinct order amongst the denominations of Christendom.

This "Higher life" theory became prominent in England about three years ago, chiefly through the ministrations of Mr. and Mrs. Pearsall Smith (formerly members of the Society of Friends) and the Rev. W. E. Boardman, all of America; and their public addresses, private reunions and published works ("Higher Christian Life," "Holiness through Faith," &c.) soon made it widely known. It attracted many disciples, enlisted the support of various ministers, and now as a school of Theology has its recognised promoters,—its "London Committee for furthering the cause of Scriptural Holiness,"—its monthly organ, "The Christian's Pathway of Power,"—and its provincial tour of Conferences and Conventions, in which (while the more generally received views of Holiness are often dwelt upon) its peculiar tenets, diluted with pleasant singing and fluent evangelical utterances, can hardly fail to be attractive.

We need carefully distinguish between those truths held by all well-instructed Christians and the tenets of this system. It is not to be denied that there is amongst believers a greater and lesser apprehension of the separating and satisfying power of Divine grace, and that the Divine fulness far exceeds the common realization of it. The possession of it is seen and the want of it lamented in the utterances of saints both of the past and present ages. This is sufficient testimony that the Church *does* believe in the fulness of Christ, the plenitude of the Spirit, and the completeness of its salvation; and a sufficient denial to the insinuation that the meaning of Scripture has been so overlooked, and the prayers of saints so ineffectual as this mysticism assumes. This mysticism!—which tried and found wanting in past times, is in its resuscitated form, proclaimed as a Divine reality in this.

ITS DIVERGENCE FROM ORTHODOX TEACHING.

This may be seen in the following, viz. :—

1. Exaggerated ideas as to the extent to which a believer can rise in conscious holiness, and freedom from internal conflict with sin.

2. A very low standard of Holiness to meet *their* comprehension of it.

3. An application to this present life of Scripture promises which belong to the future state.

4. Practical denial of the fact, that in the Christian are two principles at work—the new man and the old—flesh and spirit.

5. Contempt for sound doctrinal teaching and Church organization.

6. Misapprehension of the imputed righteousness of Christ.

7. Absurd notions as to the power of exercising faith.

8. Unwarrantable distinctions between conscious sin and perfection,—and sin and perfection as God's word explains them.

[On this point Mr. Ryle says :

"What some men call "perfection," *I* do not call "perfection." What I call "sin" *they* do not call "sin."]

This remark is true : indefiniteness on the meaning of those words often forms a safe retreat for the more moderate promoter of perfectionism, when its tenets are controverted.

ITS ASSUMPTIONS.

"Whether nakedly taught or not, Perfectionism is the keynote of the whole of Mr. Smith's system," says one ; and the statements made by its leaders as to what may be, and is attained, are such as to warrant this assertion, and either cause astonishment at their sanctity, or disgust at their presumption.

Mr. R. P. Smith writes :

"Our glorious motive power—God's own will—works in us, freed from internal opposition."

"That we should be released from the inward proneness to sin."

Another has long had Isaiah lx. 20 fulfilled in his experience, and states that " the days of his mourning are ended."

The memoir of a Dr. Upham relates how

"In the night he suddenly awoke, and saw somewhere in the heavenly regions these words, written distinctly and brightly, "Thou art my beloved son, in whom I am well pleased." He added, "These memorable words were given to me to be engraved on my heart, &c."

In the circular address of the Conference mentioned in the preface, is this sentence :

"The secret of attaining this blessing, God has graciously revealed to many dear brethren, to whom He has also *given power to impart* the knowledge to others." [!!]

These utterances (a sample of many) clash with such portions of Scripture as Rom. ix. 2 : Rom. vii. : II Cor. ii. 4 : II Thes. i. 7 : I. Peter i. 6 ; they contrast strangely with the tenor of godly experience, and they are contrary to the possibilities of our present state of existence.

The question is not what God *can* do, but what He *will* do. The following sentence, from the pen of Dr. H. Bonar, well answers many puzzling quibbles as to the present extent of sanctification :—

"I know that Christ could by one word of His power make me sinless in a moment, just as He could make this vile body incorruptible at once, without waiting for the coming resurrection. But such is not the law of the kingdom, such is not the purpose of the Father."

ITS SEDUCTIVENESS

consists very much in its *elasticity*, reaching out and adapting itself to the various contrary opinions of those who receive it: asking not that they should come out of cherished errors or embrace unpalatable truths; allowing, rather encouraging latitudinarianism in ecclesiastical matters and a wide range of personal self-pleasing: with a smile even for Romanism,—seen for instance, in the preface to Mr. Smith's selection from Faber's blasphemous Hymns; and in such remarks as this from the "Christian's Pathway of Power," which in an article on Luther and the Reformation asks :

"Was it strange that tender souls yearning for holiness, should shrink back into a Church—(the Church of Rome)—which, corrupt as it was in doctrine and ecclesiasticism, yet had sheltered some of the brightest instances of piety which the world had ever seen?"

Its seductiveness is increased by its *unfair statements of experience*: on this point one reviewer writes :

"The experience of ordinary Christians is grossly and almost absurdly misrepresented, so as to make it appear that they are consciously miserable bond slaves of sin, for ever going on in an unbroken round of sinning and repenting. The painful and ludicrous caricature is then contrasted with the glorious Scripture statements of what a believer is in the purpose of God, and what he is destined to be in glory; the awful contrast is so presented as to make superficial readers feel that all this is tremendously wrong somehow, and thus prepare them to receive the new doctrine."

One speaker at the Conference related how he asked " a minister and his wife " if such texts as 1. Peter i. 5 were true in their experience and to each question " again the answer was ' No.' " Another called on those *Christians* present who wanted " Christ as a *complete* Saviour," to stay to an after-meeting.

Let all Christians witness if at conversion they did not seek and *find* " a complete Saviour." Let them then, repel the insinuation that 1. Peter i. 5 is not the experience of ordinary Christians.

Again; many instances are cited to shew the blessedness of those who have "received" this teaching, this "second conversion." Of such cases, some are indefinite and incredible; some (giving up dancing, theatres, &c.) are results usually looked for at the *first conversion;* and others are not attributable to this system at all, but are blessed examples of the ordinary operations of the Spirit, such as Christians generally have experienced and can recognise.

WRESTING OF SCRIPTURE.

"One thing has struck me sadly in the authorized reports of the Brighton Conference,—the number of perverted passages of Scripture; and this is really the root of the whole evil. The speakers first disclaim, I might say, deride theology, and then they proceed to distort the Word of God." Dr. BONAR.

Reference to the Word of God and quotation of sets of texts, is commonly resorted to by religious theorists. It is however, especially needful to take text with context, to compare Scripture with "*all Scripture,*" so that its whole tenor may be seen instead of the unprofitable misapplication of a part.

In a manner very similar to that in which the disciples of "low experience" gather out portions of the Word that speak of trials and despondency, wherewith to strengthen their Doubting Castle, do these lay hold of texts in which holiness, completeness, perfection, &c. are mentioned, and advance them with wonderment as though almost unknown before; shunning collateral passages, and combatting those scriptures that are palpably hostile to their favorite system.

Every believer has the Spirit. Rom. viii. 9: a purified heart Acts xv. 9: is sanctified 1. Cor. vi. 11: is planted in the likeness of Christ's death, Rom. vi. 5; is crucified with Christ, Rom. vi. 6: &c. That there is a great difference as to the extent to which Christians realize and apprehend these truths and those expressed in hundreds of similar passages, none will deny; but such blessings are secured by Christ for *every saint,* and are not contingent on the uncertainties of our experience. Paul, when writing to the Corinthians, even when deploring and rebuking their unhappy conduct, reminds them of their holiness and sanctification, 1. Cor, i. 2. 30; iii. 16, 17.

Here however, the Higher Life theory takes an opposite view, and limits these truths to the attainment of *an advanced class of professors only.*

Of Romans vi. 5 : Mr. R. P. Smith writes :

"O what a lifetime of suffering some insist upon enduring in spiritual hospitals! when if they would but be 'planted in the likeness of Christ's death' they would find 'also the likeness of his resurrection.'"

In the " Secret of a Happy Life " we read :

"You may have left much to follow Christ, dear reader; you may have believed on Him, and worked for Him, and loved Him, and yet may not be like Him."

No! nor was the apostle John, whose words (1. John iii. 2) are an apt reply to many such misapplications.

A recent Higher Life publication " The Bride, the Household and the Kingdom," classifies believers under these three heads, stating that out of the Kingdom, God chooses the Household,— out of the Houschold he condescends to select the Bride. Such a fanciful conceit is in direct antagonism to the truth set forth in 1. Cor. xii. 13, &c.

To point out in detail their misuse of, and grotesque comments on portions of Scripture, would be a tedious work. It is no wonder that many, on embracing these views, find the Bible a new book, and see "a thousand meanings" in one text. The plainest Scriptures are controverted or passed by, but the 7th of Romans, where an experience *utterly incompatible with their system* is more strongly set forth than in any other part of the New Testament, is the central point of attack. Mr. Boardman calls the conflict "stuff:" another speaks of the Apostle "falling from grace and coming under the law in his practical ways;" Admiral Fishbourne, however, takes the matter in hand, and, *ex cathedra*, in a running comment *full of absurdities and incoherencies*, declares it to be the language of an " unconverted Jew."

Alas! that there should be such reckless distortion of revealed truth, which is " all plain to him that understandeth, and right to them that find knowledge."

Before leaving this subject we add

A SHORT PARAPHRASTIC COMMENT ON ROMANS VII.

The Apostle continuing his argument as to the bearing of the law and the effects of grace (Rom. i. 6) propounds three questions in this chapter, which may be taken in three sections thus, verses 1—6; 7—12 : 13—25.

First : Brethren, Roman Saints, know ye not that the law hath dominion over a person as long as he (or she) lives?

Reply. Certainly! we have a simple illustration in the case of marriage-law; by which a wife is bound to a husband, but at his death is free.

We were in the flesh, unconverted—unrenewed; then the motions of sin *working* in our members, had *scope* in manifestly wicked ways, that were plainly contrary to the law we were then bound to; so that we were condemned already, yet careless of it.

But, at the instant of our union to Christ, the law became dead to us, and we were married to another.

Note. Seeing that the law is holy, it exists *in another manner* in Christ, we serve in newness of Spirit.

Second. Is the law then the cause of sin?

Reply. No! But it makes known what *is* sin. At my conversion, for instance, when the commandment came; when I saw the comprehensive meaning of the law, I found things—such as the secret workings of concupiscence—which I had *not formerly thought to be sinful*, were exceeding sinful. Then I realized something of the *extent* of my sinfulness, long before it came into outward actions. Then I saw how holy, just, and good, was God's law.

Third. Was the law itself death to me?

Reply. No! But sin was. When I saw the holiness of God's law and **my exceeding sinfulness**, I felt that as a transgressor I was condemned.

We as believers know that the law is spiritual; and **in our** experience—in mine, for instance, I realize that I have a body of death, sold under Adam's sin (Rom. viii. 23.) These secret motions of concupiscence I allow not, yet they annoy my holy aspirations; I hate them yet, they rise. But now this sin is no longer " I ; " the " I," is the new reigning power of grace that has the law written upon its heart; and sin in me is now a condemned but struggling inmate. It is essentially evil and not good: see how it hinders the good desires of the renewed will. But now (I repeat this joyful truth) this sin is no longer " I."

I delight in the new spirit of the law, but the " law in my members "—the habit and lust of the sinful inmate,—although it cannot work freely as it once did (ver. 5), wars against me. (Gal. v. 17).

Who shall deliver me from this body of death?

God will, but the time is not yet.

The Apostle does not leave any doubt as to the condition of the soul under these experiences.

1st. Unconverted. When in the flesh (ver. 5).

2nd. Convicted. When the commandment came (ver. 9).

3rd. Saved, freed. The latter part of this chapter, as much as chap. viii., is *present* experience; and so far from the idea of "getting out of the vii. of Romans into the viii.," the declarations of the latter are based on the arguments of the former, and the earnest expectation of the one is *no nearer* perfection than the warring experience of the other. The redemption of the body is waited for (chap. viii. 23) *as much* as in chap. vii. 24.

The declaration with which chap viii. opens is inferential.

Therefore, as they who are united to Christ are not condemned (as shewn in ver. 4 of vii. chapter), I am free from the law (as shewn in ver. 6). For the law—pure and holy—was never kept by sinful men, they could not manifest its perfection; but the Son of God in a human body *did* manifest its holiness, and kept it for us.

ITS DANGERS AND TENDENCIES.

The effects of this newly promulgated notion have yet in a great measure to be manifested, but the following amongst others can already be noticed.

Self deceit and pride.

To those who have attained to the heavenly experience described by themselves, whose "days of mourning are ended," aud who are released from inward proneness to sin; the chastisement of sons (Heb. xii.), and a thorn in the flesh (II. Cor. xii.) would be unnecessary.

Again, many of the ardent admirers of this theory believe that saints may fall from grace and be finally lost. The assurance of this "Higher Life" is in direct opposition to such a creed, and to profess allegiance to contradictory doctrines is a palpable absurdity.

We may also ask if the presumption that can reckon "years without sin" would listen to I. John i. 8.?

Dr. McNeile, in a letter on this subject, after setting forth the perfection of a Christian's standing in Christ adds:

"But in the matter of the Christian's character and conduct while in unredeemed flesh, we have seen an end of all perfection, for God's commandment is exceediug broad and exceeding deep."

Perplexity and divisions.

There has always been a cherished belief that throughout the Christian dispensation, the family of God has, in the main of its experience and its teachings, been of *one heart and mind*, being led by *the same* Spirit; and sincere hearts and tender consciences are perplexed when told that so much of Christian warfare was needless, and to hear of attainments so easily gained, and the secret of perfect rest so aptly learnt, when Apostolic testimony and the recorded experience of saints, indicates a militant state, and a pilgrim journey (II. Cor. v. 4. Eph. vi. 13).

Disregard to sound doctrine and complaisance to error.

Dogmatic systems and mischievous fallacies have come in with the cry, " We are no sect," " We have no creed," and escaped detection by avoiding open statements of doctrine, until at length, when their creeds have been collated from their writings, they have been found most erroneous and unscriptural.

This thought occurs when we read in various books and hear in " Addresses on Holiness " the dubious assurance, " This is not theological ;" " I do not want to change the theological views of a single individual, &c.," or sneers at " cold creeds and mere accurate statements of doctrine." It has generally proved that such utterances conceal a dislike to sound doctrine, and are preparatory to the introduction of creeds and doctrines very unsound.

Gospel teaching *is* calculated " to change the theological views" of *all who are in error:* and the Apostolic precept to " Hold fast the form of sound words " is echoed throughout the word of God.

Good results (so easily asserted) cannot justify error even when mixed with truth ; for deviations from the revealed will of God, have a constant tendency to work their way from the more external into the most vital and essential verities of faith.

Patronized and nurtured by wealth and gentility, set forth in amiable speeches (which whilst vague and hazy, are mostly pleasant and agreeable) in its three days and ten days Conventions, where comfort and competency meet in happy freedom from daily care and earthly anxiety, can it be surprising that these ideas prosper?

ITS LITERATURE.

The different baskets of figs that Jeremiah saw did not present a greater contrast. Here is a tiny book recording the pantings of a soul after "the living Father:" there is another, the biography of somebody whose attainments are as astonishing as his conceit. Here is a chapter of sweet encouragement and healthful stimulus to present the "living sacrifice holy, acceptable unto God:" there is one, teeming with legal recipes and directions, for attaining to conscious holiness, and the self-satisfied experiences of "the Higher Life."

The out-growth of superficial experience and untried security, it commends itself to the religiousness of a luxurious age; and attaching itself to much scriptural truth it obtains credit for that which is not its own.

But *now*, where is our completeness? "In Him." There is all Christian perfection! No thought can rise to its fullness; no words can express its comprehensiveness. The soul that knows most of this will follow most closely after that holiness in word and deed which the Scripture declares to be the fruit and evidence of spiritual life. But alas! our attainment of *this* is not perfect like our participation in *that*; therefore the blood *cleanseth* because the saints are still confessing; the Spirit continues to comfort until the days of our mourning are ended; then, and not till then, released from the inward proneness to sin,—these vile bodies shall be fashioned like unto Christ's glorious body, and our perfected consciousness will awake satisfied with the likeness of God.

Christian reader, let no pleasing influence lead us on to Enchanted ground! "The assurance of faith may degenerate into an unintentional and even unsuspected presumption."

Our bodies shall be redeemed—but we wait for that adoption (Rom. viii. 23). We shall *know* when that which is perfect is come (I. Cor. xiii). We shall obtain a crown of righteousness at that day (II. Tim. iv. 8) There shall be neither sorrow nor crying, neither shall there be any more pain—when the former things are passed away (Rev. xxi. 4). We shall be like Him—when He shall appear (I. John iii. 2).

FINIS.

PRINTED BY JOHN DUTTON, TINDAL STREET, CHELMSFORD.